ENVIRONMENTAL PROTESTS

PLANET EARTH FIRST

GREENPEACE

C-BFU

BY DUCHESS HARRIS, JD, PHD

Core Library

Cover image: Greenpeace members fly a hot air balloon urging people to protect the planet.

An Imprint of Abdo Publishing
abdopublishing.com

abdopublishing.com

Published by Abdo Publishing, a division of ABDO, PO Box 398166,
Minneapolis, Minnesota 55439. Copyright © 2018 by Abdo Consulting
Group, Inc. International copyrights reserved in all countries. No part of this
book may be reproduced in any form without written permission from the
publisher. Core Library™ is a trademark and logo of Abdo Publishing.

Printed in the United States of America, North Mankato, Minnesota
092017
012018

Cover Photo: Bernd von Jutrczenka/picture-alliance/dpa/AP Images
Interior Photos: Bernd von Jutrczenka/picture-alliance/dpa/AP Images, 1; AP Images, 4–5, 7;
CQ Archive/CQ-Roll Call Group/Getty Images, 9; Leemage/Corbis Historical/Getty Images,
12–13; Gessford Picture History/Newscom, 15; RHS/AP Images, 20–21; CWH/AP Images, 23; Axel
Heimken/picture-alliance/dpa/AP Images, 26; Red Line Editorial, 28, 37; iStockphoto, 29; Henrique
NDR Martins/iStockphoto, 32–33; Ryan Rodrick Beiler/Shutterstock Images, 36

Editor: Marie Pearson
Imprint Designer: Maggie Villaume
Series Design Direction: Claire Mathiowetz
Contributor: Rebecca Rowell

Publisher's Cataloging-in-Publication Data

Names: Harris, Duchess, author.
Title: Environmental protests / by Duchess Harris.
Description: Minneapolis, Minnesota : Abdo Publishing, 2018. | Series: Protest movements |
    Includes online resources and index.
Identifiers: LCCN 2017947129 | ISBN 9781532113970 (lib.bdg.) | ISBN 9781532152856 (ebook)
Subjects: LCSH: Green movement--Juvenile literature. | Environmentalism--History--Juvenile
    literature. | Protest movements--Juvenile literature.
Classification: DDC 333.72--dc23
LC record available at https://lccn.loc.gov/2017947129

CONTENTS

CHAPTER ONE

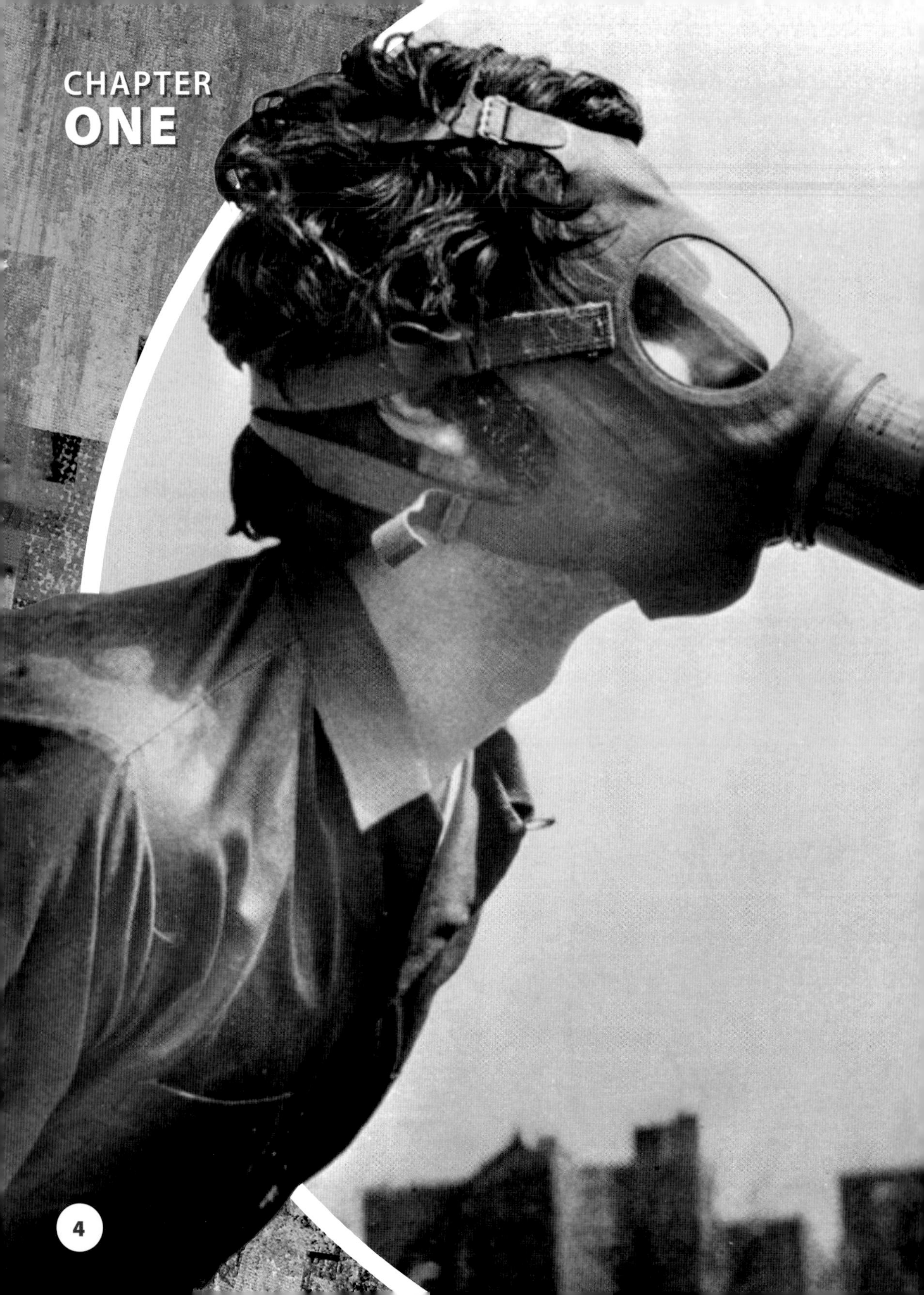

THE FIRST EARTH DAY

On April 22, 1970, millions of Americans took to the streets. Some gatherings were small. Others had crowds numbering in the thousands. All the events had the same purpose. They focused on the environment. It was the first Earth Day celebration.

In New York City, New York, at least 100,000 people gathered. Some carried protest signs. One said, "Litter Is Bitter." In the city's Union Square, people visited booths where they learned about clean air and wildlife preservation. Some people gave speeches. Mayor John Lindsay was one of the speakers.

An Earth Day participant wears a gas mask to protest air pollution.

GROWING AWARENESS

The events brought together many people. Some had already been calling attention to environmental problems. These issues included industrial pollution, toxic waste, wildlife extinction, and more. But Earth Day also drew attention from many people who weren't aware of these things. At that time, industries created massive air and land pollution. Many Americans considered these signs of success. These things meant industry was booming. But some people were becoming more aware of pollution's effects on nature.

THE IDEA

Environmental harm prompted Wisconsin senator Gaylord Nelson to create Earth Day. In 1969, he had seen the terrible effects of an oil spill in California. Oil covered the wildlife that lived in Santa Barbara Harbor. It kept birds from flying and sea otters from swimming. The bodies of dead dolphins and seals

Thousands flooded the streets in Philadelphia, Pennsylvania, for the first Earth Day.

washed ashore. Nelson wanted to take action. He would combine protesting with the growing concern for nature. He thought this might spur the environmental cause. Nelson said Earth Day would be a teaching event.

Nelson did not plan the event alone. California representative Pete McCloskey joined him. Denis Hayes helped bring the idea to life. Hayes was a student at Harvard University. He hired 85 people to advertise Earth Day events nationwide.

After Earth Day, Nelson continued to support laws that protected nature in the Senate.

9

Earth Day would take place on April 22. Nelson thought college students, who were already protesting the Vietnam War (1954–1975), would join the movement. He was right. Schools across the country joined Nelson's cause. Thousands of them planned protests.

STARTING A MOVEMENT

Earth Day 1970 was a landmark event in environmentalism. The movement has grown and found success in the decades since. The US government has created environmental

EARTH DAY SPURS POLITICAL SUPPORT

Earth Day helped launch a wave of environmental support that included politicians. Later in 1970, President Richard Nixon formed the US Environmental Protection Agency (EPA). The EPA creates, monitors, and enforces rules for controlling pollution. With the Clean Air Act of 1970, the US government took greater responsibility for limiting air pollution. This included creating national air quality standards. The Endangered Species Act of 1973 protects species that are in danger of dying out. It also protects the areas in which they live.

laws. Among them are support for clean air and animal species that are nearing extinction.

The movement has faced legal challenges. Sometimes, the government creates laws that benefit businesses more than nature. These include allowing oil companies to dig pipelines and possibly contaminate drinking water. Letting coal companies dump waste in streams is another example.

Even with challenges, environmentalists continue to fight for the planet. They are dedicated to protecting Earth and its many forms of life.

EXPLORE ONLINE

Chapter One discusses the first Earth Day. Go to the website listed below and read about Earth Day. What new information did you learn from the website? What information was similar to Chapter One?

LIVESCIENCE: EARTH DAY FACTS AND HISTORY

abdocorelibrary.com/environmental-protests

CHAPTER TWO

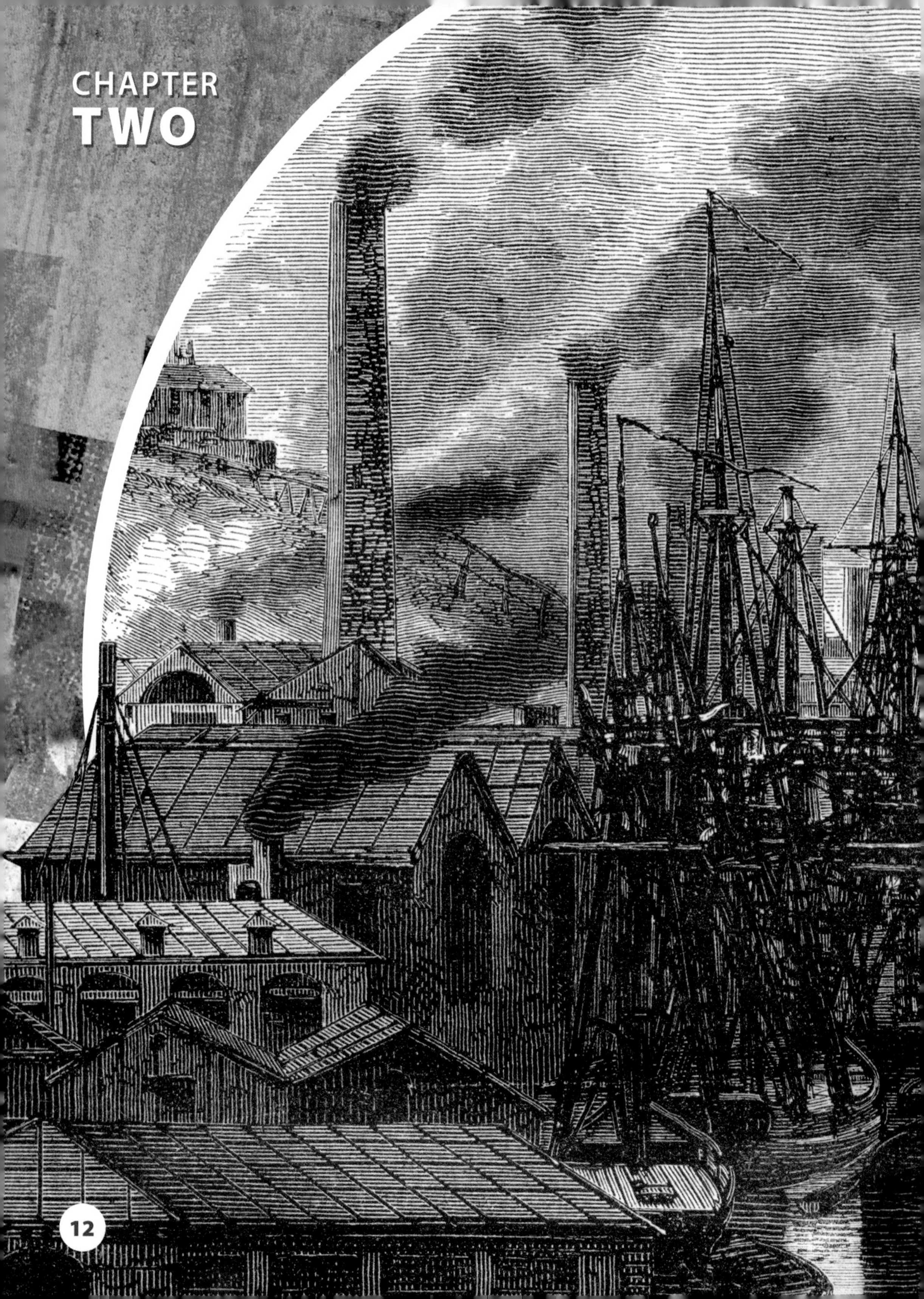

EARLY CONSERVATION

Humans' concern for nature is not new. The Maya people practiced forest conservation 3,000 years ago in what is now Guatemala. More than 1,000 years ago, Romans worried about water pollution. And a few hundred years ago, people in Europe learned that pollution could help diseases travel.

Modern environmentalism's roots began in the late 1800s. People in Europe and the United States wanted to protect natural lands. They worried about the effects of the

The air pollution caused by the Industrial Revolution in the 1800s and 1900s led to deadly smog and acid rain.

Industrial Revolution. Growing industry increased pollution. In the United States, three men were known for protecting nature. Their actions helped create protected areas of wilderness.

GIFFORD PINCHOT

Gifford Pinchot entered Yale University in 1885. He wanted to go into forestry, but the school didn't have that program. No US school had even one class in forestry. So Pinchot studied law at Yale. He then studied forestry in France. He returned to the United States and began working in forestry. He became chief of the US Division of Forestry.

In 1905, President Theodore Roosevelt made Pinchot the first head of the US Forest Service. Pinchot was the nation's first professional forester. He helped create national forests. He was part of the US Forest Service from 1905 to 1910. During that time, the number of national forests grew from 60 to 150.

Pinchot was the governor of Pennsylvania from 1923 to 1927 and from 1931 to 1935. A state park there was later named for him.

The amount of protected land in those forests more than tripled.

Pinchot supported the idea of conservation. He believed in sustainable use. He felt forests should be managed responsibly. He thought forests should be used to benefit people, such as by logging. But they should be used thoughtfully and in a way that protected nature.

JOHN MUIR

John Muir studied botany and geology at the University of Wisconsin. He traveled the country and got to know its landscapes. Forests and glaciers drew him to the Northwest and Alaska.

Like Pinchot, Muir believed the government should care for America's wilderness. But Muir wanted the land left untouched. He thought humans should leave some resources alone. Muir wrote about his ideas. His writing influenced Roosevelt.

Muir's efforts led to the creation of several national parks. These include Sequoia and Yosemite (1890), Mount Rainier (1899), and Grand Canyon (1919). Some people say Muir is the father of the National Park Service.

In 1892, Muir founded the Sierra Club. It focuses on protecting and caring for the planet. Today, it has millions of members. It is one of the largest environmental organizations.

ALDO LEOPOLD

Aldo Leopold also studied forestry. He studied it at Yale. The school had formed its forest school after Pinchot studied there. Leopold became a US Forest Service employee. He worked in the Southwest. With his influence, the US government established the Gila National Forest in New Mexico in 1924.

Later, Leopold moved to Wisconsin. He taught at the University of Wisconsin–Madison. Muir was once a student there. Leopold taught wildlife management.

He proposed a new idea called land ethic. His idea was that people should no longer view nature as something to overcome or defeat. Instead, they should care about land. They should care about people as well. Humans should work at improving their relationship with the land.

Pinchot, Muir, and Leopold held strong beliefs about humans' responsibility for nature. They influenced many people. Generations to come would be just as passionate about caring for the planet.

NATIONAL FORESTS AND NATIONAL PARKS

The United States has many preserved areas of land. Some are national parks. Others are national forests. These sites may look similar, but they are not the same. National parks and national forests both preserve nature. They have other functions too. They offer services such as recreation. National forests also provide useful resources, such as wood for lumber and grass for grazing cattle.

STRAIGHT TO THE
SOURCE

Theodore Roosevelt was another environmentalist in the early 1900s. While he was president, Roosevelt established the US Forest Service. He also created five national parks. At the time, many Americans viewed the country as having an endless supply of natural resources. Roosevelt saw the importance of conservation:

> It is also vandalism wantonly to destroy or to permit the destruction of what is beautiful in nature, whether it be a cliff, a forest, or a species of mammal or bird. Here in the United States we turn our rivers and streams into sewers and dumping-grounds, we pollute the air, we destroy forests, and exterminate fishes, birds and mammals—not to speak of vulgarizing charming landscapes with hideous advertisements. But at last it looks as if our people were awakening.

> Source: "Theodore Roosevelt and Conservation." *Theodore Roosevelt National Park*. National Park Service, n.d. Web. Accessed May 29, 2017.

What's the Big Idea?
Read the quote carefully. What is the main idea of Roosevelt's words? List two or three details he provides to support his main idea.

CHAPTER
THREE

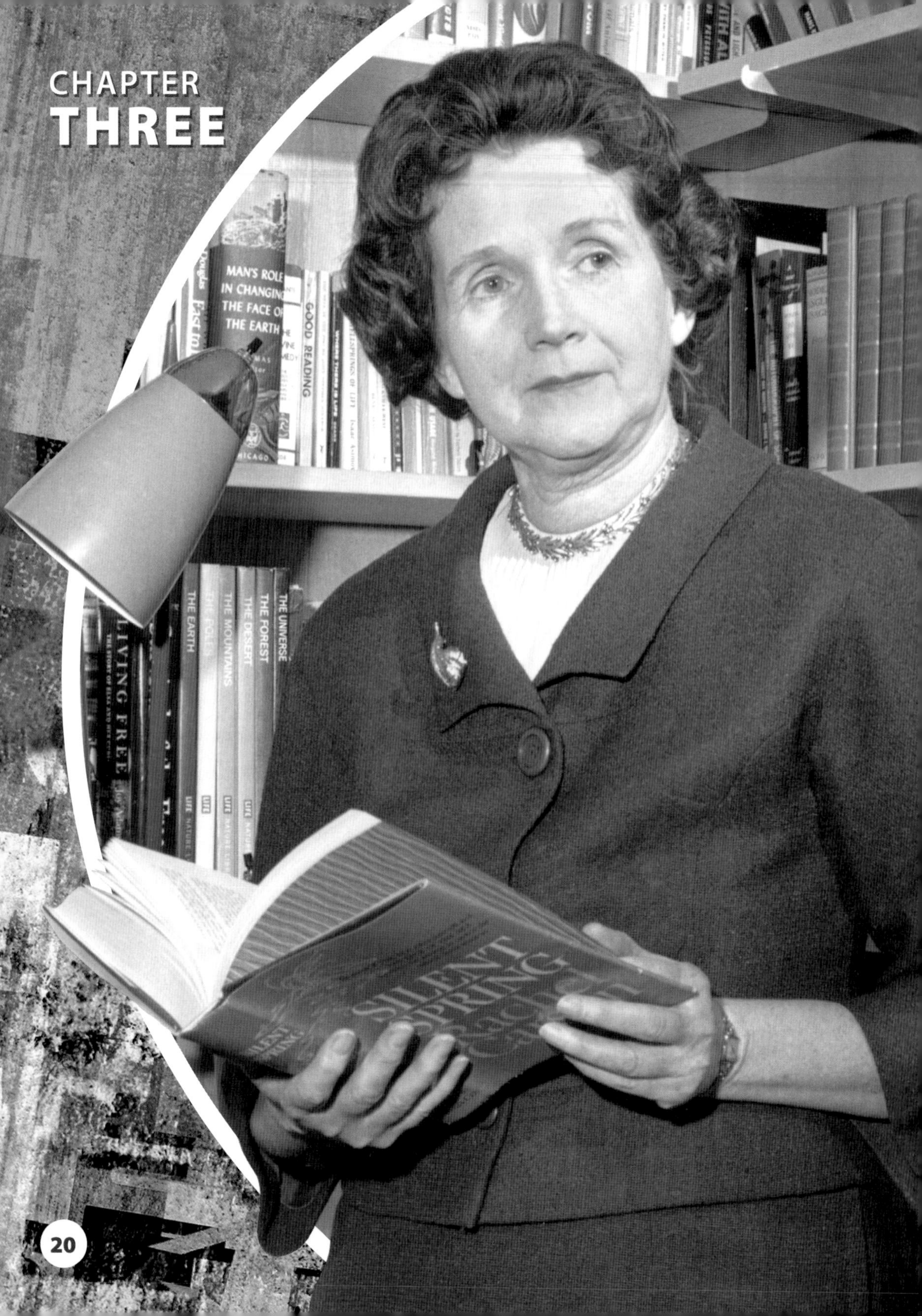

THE MOVEMENT BEGINS

After World War II (1939–1945), the US economy grew. Suburbs developed. The population and industry boomed. But this growth wasn't always good for nature.

SILENT SPRING

In 1962, biologist Rachel Carson published her book *Silent Spring*. In it, she focused on the dangers of DDT. This insecticide had been popular with farmers since the 1940s. Carson's book prompted President John F. Kennedy to take action. He asked his Science Advisory

Carson did not live to see the influence her research had. She died in 1964.

RACHEL CARSON AND ECOFEMINISM

As a scientist, Rachel Carson was certain about the dangers of DDT. Many critics didn't take her seriously. They dismissed Carson and *Silent Spring* because she was a woman. Few women were scientists at the time. Society tended to think they weren't suited for science. Attacks labeled her "hysterical" and "an uninformed woman speaking about that which she did not know."

Today, Carson serves as an inspiration for ecofeminists. Ecofeminism combines ecology and feminism. It explores the connection between women and nature, especially how men have dominated both.

Committee to investigate Carson's claims. The committee supported Carson's work. It warned about using harmful chemicals broadly. The group recommended that scientists study the possible effects to human health.

Silent Spring also made Americans think about nature in new ways. Carson shared her concern about industrial businesses. Their chemicals could prove harmful to animals and humans.

Organizations such as Environmental Teach-In used the first Earth Day to educate people about pollution and other issues.

GROWTH IN THE SIXTIES AND SEVENTIES

Concern for nature grew in the 1960s. Membership in the Sierra Club and other environmental organizations exploded. In 1960, these organizations had 123,000 total members. In 1970, the total was 819,000. Federal environmental laws also grew during this time. President Lyndon B. Johnson approved 300 laws to help nature.

ENVIRONMENTAL GROUPS STRENGTHEN THEMSELVES

During the 1970s, environmental organizations made changes. Groups became more like businesses. They hired staff members instead of relying only on volunteers. They hired lobbyists. These people promote environmental laws to politicians. Groups also hired lawyers to fight industries. Some organizations relied on scientists to argue facts in support of environmental rules. These scientists also argued against statements made by scientists working for industries. All these changes made environmental groups stronger.

Americans' support for nature was clear in 1970. Millions took part in the first Earth Day. Politicians' support was evident too. During the 1970s, the US government created agencies and laws to protect nature. This political support was partly due to the work of environmental groups. Some groups pushed for laws to protect nature. Others made sure the EPA did its job.

Environmentalists began protesting

to make their voices heard. Some people protested nuclear power plants. They were afraid of the harm a leak or radioactive waste might cause. This was especially true after one accident in 1979. A Pennsylvania nuclear plant leaked a cloud of radioactive gas that could make people and animals sick. No one was harmed. But the accident sparked fear in Americans. On May 6, 1979, as many as 125,000 people marched on Washington, DC. They protested nuclear power. Some chanted about the risks.

CHANGE IN THE EIGHTIES

The 1970s and 1980s saw a new type of environmental group. Radical organizations formed. They believed other environmental groups were working too much with governments. They had gotten away from their roots. Radical groups focused on taking action. Sometimes, this included civil disobedience and ecoterrorism.

Greenpeace activists protested a ship carrying whale meat. They hung from the ship so it could not depart.

Greenpeace is perhaps the best-known radical organization. One focus of the organization has been whaling. Greenpeace's main tactic is to get in the way. Greenpeace protestors get into inflatable rafts and position themselves between whalers and whales. In 2006, one activist even jumped on a dead whale. The man held a banner reading, "Stop Whaling." Whalers sprayed him with fire hoses.

Earth First! takes a tougher approach to protesting. In 1984, members of the group started putting metal spikes in trees that would be logged. Hitting a spike damages a saw's blade. They did this to try to stop logging.

The 1980s also brought change in the government's approach to nature. President Ronald Reagan wanted to make environmental rules less strict. This was supposed to help businesses grow. The EPA changed dramatically. It had huge cuts in funding and staff. As a result, the EPA couldn't do everything it was supposed to do.

Many Americans disliked Reagan's approach to nature. Membership in environmental organizations rose. Sierra Club grew from 180,000 members in 1980 to 630,000 in 1990. The Wilderness Society's membership jumped from 45,000 to 350,000.

Grassroots organizations also grew in the 1980s. They formed to fight local issues such as factories polluting the air or water. They were known as

PUBLIC OPINION
IN 1992

In early 1992, the Gallup organization asked some Americans what they thought about the amount of work the US government was doing to protect nature. What do you notice about the responses? How does the chart help you understand environmental activism in the United States in 1992?

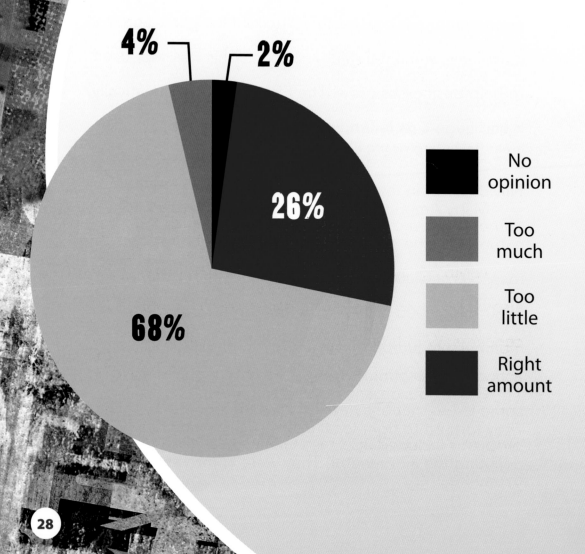

4%

2%

26%

68%

■ No opinion

■ Too much

■ Too little

■ Right amount

The Wilderness Society works to protect America's wilderness areas, including Wrangell-Saint Elias Wilderness in Alaska.

NIMBY—not in my backyard—organizations. They numbered in the thousands by the late 1980s.

NIMBY groups focused on local issues. They also helped members learn about more widespread concerns. With time, more people saw that taking action in one country wasn't always enough. To solve some issues, nations needed to work together. These problems included acid rain, climate change, and ozone loss.

GREEN IN THE NINETIES

April 22, 1990, marked the 20th anniversary of Earth Day. That year, the celebration went global. Approximately 200 million people in 141 countries participated in Earth Day events. The worldwide celebration helped bring attention to environmental issues.

For some people, environmental concerns weren't getting enough attention. Some environmentalists wanted a political party focused on nature. In 1996, the National Association of State Green Parties (NASGP) formed. That year, the party endorsed Ralph Nader for president. He became the first Green Party candidate for US president. Winona LaDuke ran as his vice presidential candidate. LaDuke is an Anishinaabe Native American activist. She had protested the act of cutting down young and old trees to make paper. She had influence in Native American communities. The pair lost the election. They ran again in 2000 and also lost. But other members of the party did win local elections.

STRAIGHT TO THE
SOURCE

April 22, 1995, marked Earth Day's 25th anniversary. That day, Gaylord Nelson spoke about the danger of continuing to use natural resources thoughtlessly:

Do we who are here today owe anything to future generations of people and other living things? . . .

Increasingly, we have come to understand that the wealth of the nation is its air, water, soil, forests, minerals, rivers, lakes, oceans, scenic beauty, wildlife habitats and biodiversity. Take this resource base away and all that is left is a wasteland.

Source: "Environment. Population. Sustainable Development: Where Do We Go from Here?" *Gaylord Nelson and Earth Day.* Nelson Institute for Environmental Studies, 2017. Web. Accessed June 27, 2017.

Changing Minds

Nelson asked listeners if people owe anything to future generations. Read the quote carefully. Take a position in response to Nelson's question, then imagine that your best friend has the opposite opinion. Write a short essay trying to change your friend's mind. Detail your opinion and your reasons for it. Provide facts and details that support your reasons.

CHAPTER FOUR

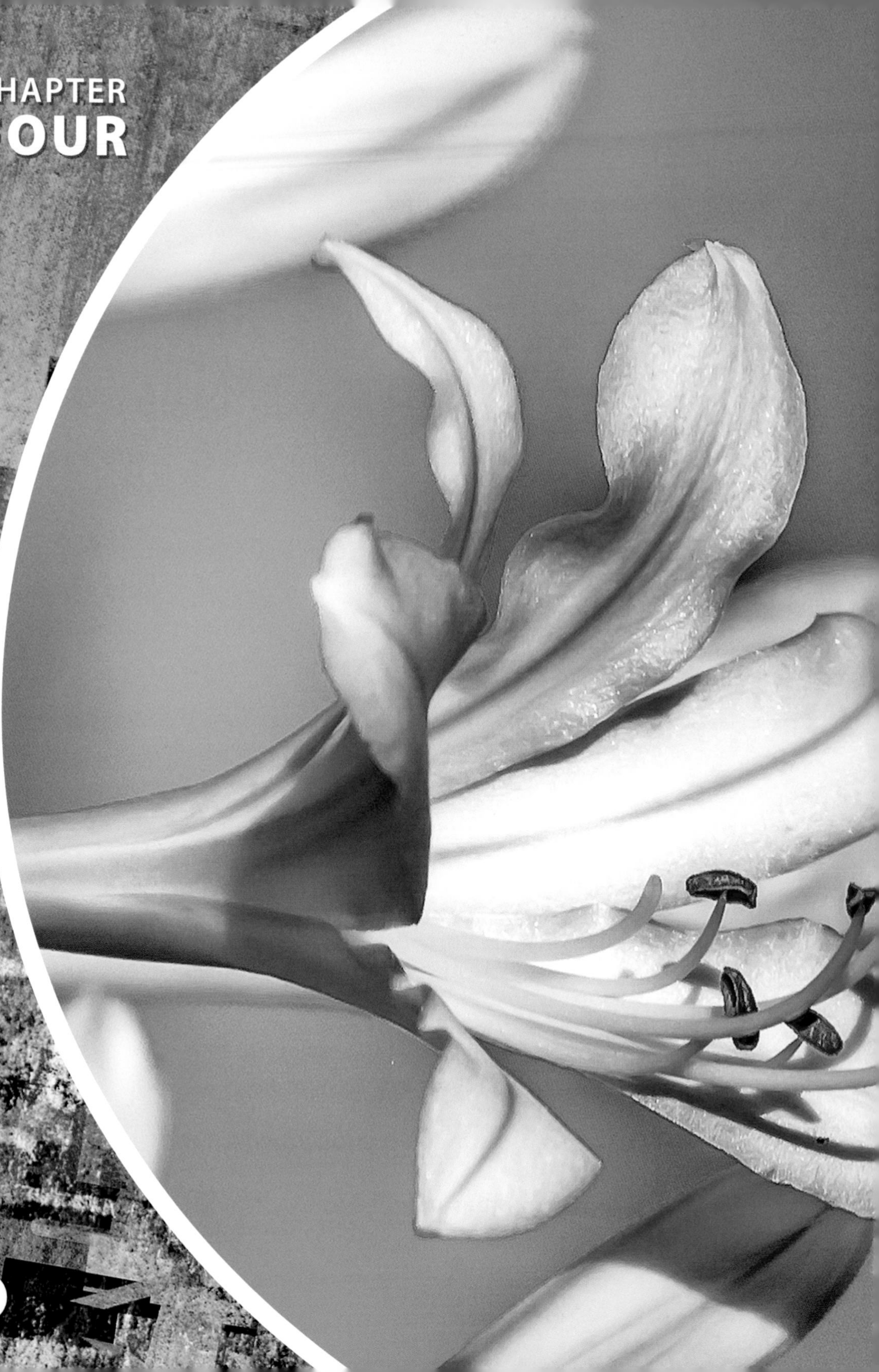

SAVING EARTH TODAY

In 2016, the United Nations released a report about the environment. It showed a decline in several areas. These included biodiversity, land quality, the amount of water, and the amount of arctic sea ice. Climate change is a major concern. Other current global environmental issues include pollution, deforestation, and extinction.

In the United States, some important animal populations, such as the bee

Bees help plants reproduce by carrying pollen from one flower to another.

NATIVE AMERICANS PROTEST PIPELINE

In 2016 and 2017, Native Americans protested development of the Dakota Access oil pipeline. Its route through North Dakota would pass through the Standing Rock Sioux reservation, beneath Lake Oahe. The lake provides drinking water to the reservation and the neighboring Cheyenne River Sioux reservation. The pipeline would put the safety of the drinking water at risk. Protestors faced rubber bullets and water cannons. They were fighting for their health and their land. They protested outside the White House in March 2017. But President Donald Trump gave oil companies approval to build the pipeline.

population, have been declining. Bees help plants reproduce. Plants provide food for people and many animals. Individuals and organizations are working to fix these issues.

ENVIRONMENTAL JUSTICE

Today, activists in environmentalism also focus on race. For decades, environmental issues have affected minorities more than or in different ways than white middle- and upper-class Americans.

Research shows sites that harm nature are often located in poor areas. And people of color often live in these areas.

Access to clean water is an issue too. African Americans are twice as likely as whites to live in houses with poor plumbing and without drinkable water. Minorities also have greater exposure to nitrogen dioxide. Cars and factories create this gas. It can cause breathing problems.

One person fighting for environmental social justice is Anthony Kapel "Van" Jones. He is a civil rights activist. He supports nature. He believes civil rights and environmental quality are linked. He created Green for All. The organization tries to build a green economy that includes minorities. A green economy prospers industrially while caring for nature. Green for All wants that economy to help nature. It also tries to help those who live in poverty get out of it.

In 2009, Jones worked under President Barack Obama, directing government funding for green jobs.

GEORGE W. BUSH

Politicians also continue to influence environmentalism. The US presidents in office since 2000 have approached environmentalism differently. George W. Bush was president from 2001 to 2009. He made some environmental advances. In 2009, he created a national monument in the ocean waters near Hawaii. It protects a variety of ocean life. But overall, environmentalists think Bush pushed the movement in the wrong direction.

LIVING AT
RISK

In 2014, more than 130 million Americans lived close to vulnerability zones. These are areas where residents could face the risk of a dangerous chemical disaster. This chart shows what percentages of African Americans and white people make up the population as a whole as compared to the percentages living in vulnerability zones. What do you notice about the percentage differences? Do you think this information supports or refutes the idea that minorities are at greater risk for experiencing environmental harm?

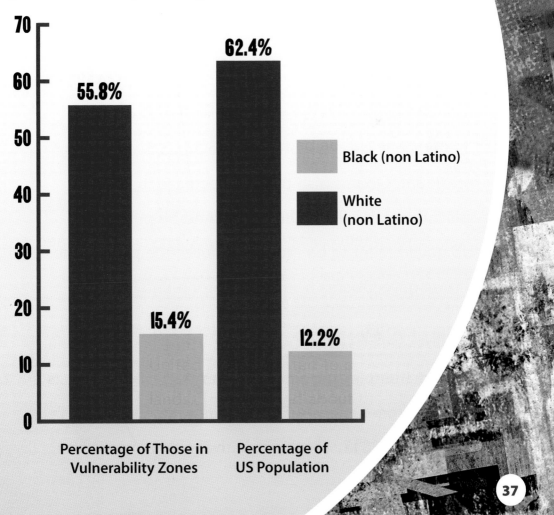

- Black (non Latino)
- White (non Latino)

55.8%
62.4%
15.4%
12.2%

Percentage of Those in Vulnerability Zones

Percentage of US Population

They criticized his administration's lack of action to prevent climate change.

BARACK OBAMA

Bush's successor was very different. Barack Obama was president from 2009 to 2017. During his last two years, he focused on the environment. Climate change was a priority. He promoted the Clean Power Plan. It would cut US power plant emissions.

America's land and water were important to Obama too. He created or increased the size of 34 national monuments. He did more in these areas than any other president. Obama also tried to decrease the oil and gas industries' effects on nature. And he pushed the US government to be more mindful of the planet. These efforts gave Obama a strong environmental legacy.

DONALD TRUMP

Donald Trump's environmental approach has greatly differed from Obama's. Trump's first day in office was January 20, 2017. That day, the website for the White

House changed. The new text reflected Trump's beliefs and plans. It included his goal of cutting back the power of the EPA. And every mention of fighting climate change had disappeared. This included information about the effects of global warming.

Trump made Scott Pruitt, then Oklahoma's attorney general, the head of the EPA. Pruitt once sued the EPA.

Pruitt also does not agree with research about climate change. He disagrees with scientists who say that humans are the biggest cause of this global problem.

Trump has also undone much of Obama's environmental work. In February 2017, he canceled tougher rules Obama had just approved before leaving office. They were rules on dumping mining waste into rivers and streams. Trump felt disposing of waste safely would cost businesses too much money.

MARCH FOR SCIENCE

Many people approved of Trump's ideas and actions. Many did not. Some who did not took action. On April 22, 2017, people worldwide marched for the planet, for science, and against Trump. It was Earth Day. Thousands of protestors took to the streets. Supporters gathered in cities across the country. The main march was in Washington, DC. Some protest signs read, "There Is No Planet B."

Protestors also marched in Australia, Japan, New Zealand, and South Africa. They marched in Europe. They couldn't undo what Trump had done. However, they could show their disapproval.

It was 47 years after the first Earth Day. And people did just as Nelson had hoped when he came up with the idea for the event. His idea lives on. With the dedication and action of environmentalists, Earth and its many forms of life will live on as well.

FURTHER EVIDENCE

Chapter Four introduced some actions recent presidents have taken regarding nature. What was the main point of this chapter? What evidence is included to support this point? Go to the website below and explore information about how the Trump administration is affecting nature. Does the information support any of the chapter's main points? Does it add a new point?

NATIONAL GEOGRAPHIC: A RUNNING LIST OF HOW TRUMP IS CHANGING THE ENVIRONMENT

abdocorelibrary.com/environmental-protests

FAST FACTS

- Environmentalism takes action in support of the environment. It encompasses many areas, including air, water, soil, population, wildlife, energy, and animals. Environmentalists use different tactics, including protests, education, and lobbying. Some use ecoterrorism or risk physical harm and even death by protesting.

- Key players include President Theodore Roosevelt, Gifford Pinchot, John Muir, Aldo Leopold, Rachel Carson, President Lyndon B. Johnson, and President Barack Obama.

- In 1962, Rachel Carson's book *Silent Spring* brought many Americans' attention to the environment.

- The first Earth Day took place in the United States on April 22, 1970.

- President Richard Nixon established the Environmental Protection Agency in December 1970.

- Earth Day became a global celebration on April 22, 1990, its 20th anniversary.

- President Barack Obama created a strong environmental legacy while president from 2009 to 2017.

IMPORTANT
DATES

Late 1800s and early 1900s
Gifford Pinchot, John Muir, and Aldo Leopold
advocate for conservation or preservation of resources.

1962
Rachel Carson's book *Silent Spring* is published.

1970
The first Earth Day takes place in the United States on
April 22.

1970
President Richard Nixon establishes the Environmental
Protection Agency in December.

2009–2017
President Barack Obama creates a strong environmental
legacy while president.

2017
President Donald Trump begins undoing Obama's
work, including his environmental achievements. On
April 22, protestors around the world march for the
planet and for science.

STOP AND
THINK

Tell the Tale
Chapter One of this book discusses the first Earth Day. Imagine you are one of the millions of people who participated. Write 200 words about what you saw and heard that day. What did you learn about the environment?

Surprise Me
Chapter Three describes the evolution of environmentalism. After reading this book, what two or three facts about environmentalism did you find most surprising? Write a few sentences about each fact. Why did you find each fact surprising?

Dig Deeper
After reading this book, what questions do you still have about environmentalism? With an adult's help, find a few reliable sources that can help you answer your questions. Write a paragraph about what you learned.

GLOSSARY

biodiversity
having a variety of animal and plant life

conservation
the careful control of the way a resource is used to avoid too much of it being used and to protect the environment

ecoterrorism
an act of violence and destruction done for the cause of environmentalism

insecticide
a chemical that kills insects

ozone
a chemical that occurs in the layer of the atmosphere that protects Earth from harmful sunlight

preservation
the act of setting aside and protecting a natural area and not letting people or industries use its resources, such as trees for lumber

reproduce
to have offspring

sustainable use
the practice of using natural resources in a careful and controlled way to maintain biodiversity and protect the environment

ONLINE
RESOURCES

To learn more about environmental protests, visit our free resource websites below.

Core Library
CONNECTION
FREE! COMMON CORE MULTIMEDIA RESOURCES

Visit **abdocorelibrary.com** for free Common Core resources for teachers and students, including vetted activities, multimedia, and booklinks, for deeper subject comprehension.

Booklinks
NONFICTION NETWORK
FREE! ONLINE NONFICTION RESOURCES

Visit **abdobooklinks.com** for free additional online weblinks for further learning. These links are routinely monitored and updated to provide the most current information available.

LEARN
MORE

Rowell, Rebecca. *Rachel Carson Sparks the Environmental Movement.* Minneapolis, MN: Abdo Publishing, 2016.

Spalding, Maddie. *Yosemite National Park.* Minneapolis, MN: Abdo Publishing, 2017.

ABOUT THE
AUTHOR

Duchess Harris, JD, PhD
Professor Harris is the chair of the American Studies Department at Macalester College.
The author and coauthor of four books (*Hidden Human Computers: The Black Women of NASA* and *Black Lives Matter* with Sue Bradford Edwards, *Racially Writing the Republic: Racists, Race Rebels, and Transformations of American Identity* with Bruce Baum, and *Black Feminist Politics from Kennedy to Clinton/Obama*), she has been an associate editor for *Litigation News*, the American Bar Association Section's quarterly flagship publication, and was the first editor-in-chief of *Law Raza Journal*, an interactive online race and the law journal for William Mitchell College of Law.

She has earned a PhD in American Studies from the University of Minnesota and a Juris Doctorate from William Mitchell College of Law.

INDEX